Productivity

Powerful Techniques, Hacks and Habits for Small Business Owners!

Contents

The trademarks that are used are without any consent, and the publication of the trademark is without permission or backing by the trademark owner. All trademarks and brands within this book are for clarifying purposes only and are the owned by the owners themselves, not affiliated with this document.

Chapter 1. The Busy Life of a Small Business Owner

If you own and operate a small business you understand that life is busy. It's more than just the demands of your business; it's the demands on your time, your life, and your income. There is a lot riding on what you can accomplish in a day, and if you don't have time management practices in place along with proper organizational systems, there is a greater potential for failure in one or all of these areas.

It may sound daunting to think that you may have missed a vital part of running your business. The thought that this could affect your future success is also a consideration, but the good news is that it's not too late. There are things you can put into place now that will help turn the tide. They won't be overnight fixes, though some will lend you immediate results, but they are instead helpful for a type of mental shift. A reorienting of goals, processes, and priorities that will affect the trajectory of your current situation, leading you to a healthier business perspective and an efficient overall work attitude.

In this book we'll take a look at the "whys" to small business time management and organization as well as "tips and tricks" for reorienting your business.

We'll cover topics like:

- Time management killers
- Organizational skills for office, work, and home space

- Daily commute tips
- Making the best of communicating with your staff and customers
- Systems to put in place to free up time

These and many other aspects of small business time management and organization will be discussed all with the desire to create a well-working, thought out plan for you and your business.

This book isn't something that will transform your business immediately. Most of the issues and solutions we'll discuss take time to put into place. Bad habits are formed quickly, but they are even harder to break. For small business owners, these habits may have come from a desire to do good, but the outcome proved to be less than what was hoped for. In any event, we encourage you to take into account the fact that these tips and tricks will need to be adapted to you and your business model. You may be a small business with no employees or a small business with ten employees. No matter you situation, take into account the principle behind each tip and trick mentioned, and ask yourself if there is a way that you can implement that principle into your schedule or routine.

Living Life as a Small Business Owner

Is it possible to live a fulfilling life as a small business owner?

This question is important to answer for yourself as a small business owner because the answer to it will determine a few things.

1. The importance you place on your role as a small business owner
2. The amount of time you are willing to invest in your small business

3. The quality of life you allow yourself to have as a small business owner
4. Your attitude toward your small business

If the answer is "No"

If you believe that it is *not* possible to live a fulfilling life as a small business owner you are likely placing too much importance on your role as a small business owner, and not enough on the quality of your own life. You likely feel stressed, anxious, and potentially haunted by your business and its day-to-day actives and success.

This type of attitude toward your business is, of course, dangerous, but not for the reasons you would initially think. It actually affects your business success, not just *you* as the owner.

How? Well, first off, if you are a stressed out, over-worked, anxious business owner, your employees, your family and friends, and your customers will feel this. Working or shopping in this type of environment will adversely affect not only you, but also those around you.

Employees

Should you have employees, they will be less likely to go above and beyond for you as a boss due to the fact that they cannot (or do not want to) relate to you. Those under stress can act rashly, demand things, and impose their stress on others. No one generally enjoys being around these type of people. This type of stress then transfers to the employee creating stress in them. It's a dangerous cycle.

Family and Friends

Though personal, we must take into account
the full perspective of a person. You are not just
a stand alone being. Everyone likely has
someone in their life, whether family or friends,
who will affect you and be affected by you.
Living in a constantly stressful state will have
adverse affects on those you love and care
about in your life. This, like the employee
scenario, is a dangerous cycle that will only end
in anguish and argument most of the time.

Consider the idea that, though it is good to
separate your family life from your business
life, you remain the "constant" in that scenario.
You cannot avoid being affected by your
business, but you can work against carrying
that stress home with you, as you would avoid
bringing tension from home to work. The
balance in this is keeping your perspective
straight with regards to work and home life.

Maintain healthy boundaries for work and be "all there" when at home or with friends.

Customers

Last, but potentially most important to a small businessperson, is the affect a stressful environment will have on your customers. A business owner who constantly lives an over stressed life (likely due to lack of organization and poor time management skills) will find their patience short, their understanding limited, and their customer service abilities to be depleted. It takes a lot of patience and understanding to deal with angry customers in order to give them the best customer service possible. If you are at the end of your rope emotionally, you will be less likely to sympathize with someone who is unhappy with his or her service.

As a businessperson, it is crucial that you put as much effort into having excellent customer service as you would an excellent product. Your product will say a lot, but happy customers will tell everyone they know about your service or product just as they will if they are unhappy.

If the answer is "yes"

If you *do* agree that it is possible to live a fulfilling life as a small business owner then you have likely answered differently to the questions above. You understand the importance of your role in your small business, but you are more open handed about it. You allot your time appropriately with regards to your business and your personal life. You make time and provision for yourself with regards to rest and relaxation. You also have an open and hopeful attitude toward your business.

This type of attitude is infectious and is likely present in successful small business ventures. It may seem like a small thing, but attitude really is everything. It will show itself most plainly in the lives of your employees, those you care about, and your customers.

Employees

A small business owner and boss who thinks that there is more to life than their business recognizes the importance of their employees lives in the context of a successful working relationship. This doesn't mean catering to the employee's every need or whim. However, it does mean having an understanding attitude, allowing procedures and practices to be in place for the benefit of the employee as well as proper preparation and training for those employees. When an employee is on board with the vision of the business and takes a vested interested in the product or service being offered, they are one of the best assets you will have.

Family and Friends

Part of a fulfilling lifestyle in association with being a small business owner is having time to spend with your family and close friends. There are sacrifices that need to be made in order to be successful, but they shouldn't be completely at the expense of those you care about. Your friends and family are your support system and will be there through it all. Give them the respect and attention they deserve, though make sure to communicate to them that you will need to make some sacrifices, especially at the beginning stages of your business (or enacting a new business plan).

Customers

Living a fulfilled life as a small business owner will also be reflected to your customers. In the same way a negative interaction due to stress will adversely affect your customer's experience, a positive interaction will have numerous benefits. A customer loves to see a business owner who is proud of their product or service and who has a genuine passion for what they do. Business owners who have a balanced approach to running their small business typically have more patience and understanding toward their customers and are more likely to go above and beyond for a great product or service.

Chapter 2. The Why: Why Organization Is Important For Small Business Owners

The first question that must be answered is this: Is organization important for small business owners?

The answer to this question is a resounding *yes*. This is likely the reason you are reading this book, but before we discuss practical ways to attack the lack of organization in your small business, we must identify a few things.

Areas in Need of Organization

There are many areas in your business that fall in the category of needing organization:

- Business plan and goals
- Communication (client, customer service, employee etc.)
- Marketing and promotion
- On-site (store, office, work area etc.)
- Finances

This isn't a complete list and things will vary depending on the type of business you run, but each of these areas require some type of organization that is understandable to all who are involved in dealing with that area. We'll discuss more about how to put these things in to practice and what organization can look like for each, but first let's see why their organization is important.

Business plan and future goals

Depending on where you are at in your small business venture, you will either have this in place or be beyond the point of referencing your initial business plan. Things do change, and that makes it even more important to schedule in time to reevaluate these plans and goals.

With regards to a business plan and your future goals, these are a great way for your business to remain organized on a single point of focus. This isn't to say only one thing is important for your business, but it is to hone in on the *most important* factor of your business. This is likely a question you will be asked regarding your branding, but it is also important for the organization of your business.

Ask yourself:

- What is the most important aspect of my business (product or service)?
- What makes me the best at what I do (providing this product or service)?
- What makes my business stand out?
- What are my goals for the future?

In terms of organization, the answers to these questions will help you prioritize the focus of your business. Prioritizing is a crucial skill you need to master when considering decisions about your business, plans involving you or your business, and programs and scheduling with regards to your business.

Discovering the "heart" of why you do what you do allows you to reorient everything around that heart. If you have a desire to do something, your first step is to reference your stated "heart" and see if the idea falls in line with this. If so, then move ahead. If not, either put it aside for the future or completely move on.

You may find that you come to a decision like this and realize that you *want* it to fit within the confines of what you find important for your business even if this idea or project doesn't. At that point, you may need to evaluate whether it's time for you to go back and reassess your initial business plan and goals.

This is all part of your businesses organization because it provides the foundation to your small business. The reasons behind your business constitute guidelines through which all of your business decisions will be made. Think of them as the organizational boxes you fit everything into.

Communication

Communication is second in importance when thinking through why (and how) your business must be organized. If you cannot accurately communicate things about your business (plan, facts and figures), or to your employees and/or customers, then your business is less likely to succeed.

Your business plan: Being able to put your business plan into writing in order to have something solid to refer back to is crucial. This goes back to the first point and the idea of the "heart" of your business. Have this in writing and refer back to it often when making decisions or moving forward.

What you're about: Communication comes in many forms. When communicating to your clients or prospective customers, you need to be able to accurately portray your business through words. This means having a document(s) on hand that lays out the essentials of your business with easily understandable taglines, points of interest, and frequently asked questions.

Customer Communication: No one likes to feel as if they have fallen through the cracks. Follow up is extremely important with customers, no matter what business you are in, and you need to have a way to track this communication to be sure you've put forth your best effort to establishing a great customer service experience.

Employee Communication: Communication with your employees (should you have any) is also extremely important. You must be able to communicate to your employees in an understandable, clear, and organized way to outline their responsibilities, your expectations, and policies and procedures you'd like put in place.

Marketing and promotion

This aspect deals with two types of organization. You must physically be organized with your marketing and promotional materials to have easy and quick access to them, but you must also have intangible organization of ideas and schedules.

In order to have a strong social media presence and a good marketing platform, you must be consistent with posts, sharing information and ideas, and easy access for your clients or potential customers to find what they need to find. This means functional organization of your website, schedules, and calendars for posting in addition to many other areas that will affect your business and its online presence.

On-site

This is the most tangible aspect to organization. Whether this is your home, office, workspace, or storefront, organization is key to creating a stress free environment that is conducive to work. You may not have a natural inclination to keep things clean and organized, but it will be to your benefit if you take the time to put systems into place that will allow you to work well in your environment. This is also important for others who may be hired to work for you.

The idea of having an organized workspace isn't just for aesthetics. You will function at a higher capacity when you are able to find what you need right away. Organization will also cut down on over spending on supplies you already have in addition to creating a space where your employees or helpers can work along side you or without you, no matter the task.

Financial

In the financial area, you must be organized not only so that you can find or reference what you need, but so that your CPA or financial assistant has access to the files, forms, and information that they need. It is also an area of tangible organization, but having things in place will free you up in the long run. No one enjoys searching through stacks of paper or piles of receipts come tax day. Instead, putting something into place that helps you get organized and stay organized early will pay off very quickly.

The additional bonus here is an eye to detail. The financial side to your business is very important. If you hire this out to someone they will likely come in with their own form of organization. If you do this yourself, you will need to learn the best way to stay organized. Either way, we recommend you have a hand in your financial organization to monitor how it is handled. It's not an area you should try to control if you aren't well versed in it, but it is something you should be informed on no matter the situation.

Organizational Styles

There are many styles of organization. The *best* type of organization is the one that works for you. In deciding this, you must factor in a few things:

- What space do I have for organization?

- Who needs to understand the organization?
- How much can I afford to spend on organization?
- What will save me time and effort?

As you factor in these things you'll start to see that the answer to each of these questions plays a different role. When you think about the space you are organizing, you must consider what fits and what doesn't. There may be several spaces such as the business or storefront itself, your personal space, storage areas, and then digital space.

When you've deiced what needs to be organized and where, you will need to decide who needs to understand this organization. If you are the sole employee, you alone are responsible for the organized spaces. This simplifies things because you will naturally gravitate to your own type of organizational reasoning. It requires more thought when you consider employees who will need to understand your layout and organizational reasoning.

The type of organization you do can be as little as file folders to as great as installing moveable systems for files. This is determined by your budget, space available, and the amount of things that must be organized. On a smaller budget, you will want to invest in heavy-duty cardboard boxes, file folders, and a sharpie. With an increased budget, you can install file cabinets with special hanging file folders along with the use of a label maker to create legible labels for every area.

The consideration for organization of your work and office space boils down to one concept: saving you time and energy. We'll talk more about time management later, but organization is one way that can save you and your business great amounts of time, which equals money.

Creating spaces that maximize organizational potential while allowing you to access everything you need in a short amount of time will not only save you frustration, it will also smooth out processes in your business freeing you up to focus on more important things.

Delegating Organization

We've discussed how important organization is to your small business. There are times when you may become overwhelmed by the task of getting organized, which is a perfect time for you to consider either hiring out this task or asking a friend for help.

There are positives and negatives to delegating organization. On the negative side, having someone else organize for you is pointless unless they are able to instruct you on where they put things and why. The *why* is very important here because not only do you want to be able to find your information, but you should also see this as a learning experience. Someone who is gifted in organization has perfected a method. By their explanation, you can then learn and adapt their way to your own. This becomes difficult only if what they have done doesn't logically make sense to you. It is wise to discuss organizational styles before having someone step into your space to organize it. Make sure that you are on the same page.

On the positive side though, delegating the organization of your space will free you up to focus on what needs your attention most in your business. This will also allow you to play to the strengths of your organizer. It is even better if they are already your employee and the organizational side can become part of their job responsibility. Again though, be sure to fully understand their organizational thought process and/or have them write it out so that, should they leave (vacation or permanently) you have something to refer to.

Staying Organized

Remaining organized must be prioritized in your small business plan. This isn't a "fix it and forget" it issue. It is sometimes a daily routine. That may sound exhausting, but the more easily associated you are with your organizational systems and where things are located, the easier it will be.

We recommend setting aside the last fifteen or twenty minutes of your day to "re-set". This looks like cleaning up your desk area, restocking or arranging shelved items, and filing papers away. Don't spend more on this than you should. If you are diligent to keep up on filing and organization daily, you won't find yourself behind at the end of the week and in need of staying late.

Organization is key to the success of any small business. It will initially take time up front, though this will depend on how much you have to organize, but in the end you will find it more than worth the effort. The ease with which you can find and replace items, paperwork, and even supplies will cut back on the stress of searching for the things you need.

As a healthy start (or re-start) to any business, take at least a day—or a weekend—to re-set the life of your business and focus on organization. Use the tips and tricks mentioned in the next chapter to get you started.

Chapter 3. Small Business Organization Tips and Tricks

We've identified why organization is necessary and have pointed out areas that are typically in need of organization for small businesses. This section will talk about practical ways with which to stay organized in these areas, and systems that can be put into place for the future of your business. These systems are helpful because they can grow and change with your business and number of employees.

Think of these tips and tricks not as a cure-all to your businesses organizational issues, but more like a splint to a broken arm. You must set the break and then hold it in place for the healing to begin. The same can be said for a "broken" businesses – businesses without organization or helpful systems. They must be re-set by going through the sometimes painful process to identify where they aren't functioning well, and then put back into pace. This may take drastic action in some cases, and in others, just a small fix here and there. Then, the splint is used to keep the new procedures and practices in place. They hold the changes in place, give you ways to shore up your business, and help you stick to the plan you implement.

As we've said, these systems aren't the cure, but they help you work toward an end goal with the hopes of seeing growth and healing toward better organization in your business.

Business plan and future goals

This step is usually taken care of by the time your business is in full swing, at least the planning portion of it, but if you are getting ready to re-shape your business organizationally, you may consider reevaluating your business plan as well. This doesn't mean you will throw out everything you've done and replace it with all new systems, only that you will take into account the new types of organization you'll implement and make adjustments where necessary.

Organizing Your Business Plan

Depending on the type of business you have (or wish to start) your business plan will look differently in some aspects.

Across the board you will take a look at:

- The intent or purpose of your business

- Description of your Business
- Market Analysis
- Overall Plan of Action
- Finances

The more understandable and up-to-date your business plan is, the more focused you can be. Think of your business plan as the manual to your business. You are writing out the focus, intent, and "big idea" behind everything you do.

Smart Idea: Be able to boil your business down into a one-sentence idea ("heart") or tagline that easily conveys your business to someone. Don't use a lot of buzzwords or generalizations. Keep this clear, concise, and effective.

Organizing your Future Goals

To begin organization of these things, sit down and establish your future goals. If you already have this document, pull it out and evaluate if your goals are still true. If so, asses how far along you are, how long it has taken you to get there, and where you still need to improve in order to reach your goals.

We recommend starting with less-defined, long-term goals and then working your way back to current, achievable goals. The idea here is to frame your goal sheet with a distant or "big picture" overview first. You can be somewhat specific with your long-term goals, but as you write out steps to work toward those goals, become more and more detailed. By the time you are working on your goals for the next six months to a year, you should have very clearly defined, actionable steps to take working toward those goals.

After you have these goals outlined, we recommend taking the time to input them into your business calendar. Some steps and goals may not be achievable in the timeframe you allot for them, just as some things may be accomplished in a shorter timeframe. Either way, keeping a record of your successfully reached goals and missed goals is very important. Use this data to hone and shape your next goals for the future. You can find more specified steps for goal planning in Chapter 6.

Smart Idea: Once you've identified your actionable steps for the next six months to a year, plan out regular check-up meetings (either alone or with staff) to go over your progress. Like health and wellness checkups, they are necessary for the health of your business.

Communication

As we've mentioned, communication is quintessential to the success of your business. Organizing this communication is just as important.

Consider these types of communication:

- Advertisement
- Email
- Phone calls/text messages
- Social Media
- Employee
- Customers (customer service)
- Vendors/businesses

Each of these different areas necessitates a slightly different type of communication. You won't communicate to an employee in the same way you will a customer, just as you won't communicate via email in the same way you would on social media.

Voice

You may not realize it, but written communication has a tone to it. In the study of English, it is called this the voice. The tone of voice with which you write is extremely important for many reasons, though it may change depending on who you are communicating with.

For example, a more relaxed (yet still businesslike) tone of voice is appropriate when communicating with your employees, yet a businesslike and professional voice is necessary when dealing with customers. We see tone of voice becoming a selling point for some companies that rely on whit and fast-paced humor to make their products accessible and fun to consumers. Don't underestimate the power the written word has on your customers.

Consistency

This point falls in line with tone of voice in your writing. Make sure you decide on a consistent voice for all of your written communication. This may mean hiring one person to write for you (at least with regards to marketing and social media) in order to keep the voice consistent. The same can be said for communication with your employees. You set the tone and type of communication and they will follow that.

This is an important point when considering organization because, should you prefer to organize your written communication online, you may require your employees to email you their vacation requests, sick notices, or special requests so that you can keep track. On the other hand you may desire a quick text so that you can input it into an Evernote document or directly on your calendar. Whatever you choose, be sure to clearly communicate this with your employees to avoid any type of confusion.

*Smart Idea: Use special applications like Evernote or Google Calendar when organizing your business. The best types of apps are those that automatically update from your phone to your computer and tablet. This way, when you input something on one device, you can be sure it will transfer to the rest. This saves you time and energy by not having to input things more than once!

Timeliness

The point of organizing your communication is to move toward timeliness. The basis for customer service rests on the immediate and comprehensive satisfaction of your customers or clients. When someone sends in an email requesting help or information, you must have a system in place to track that email or communication. This may be a simple spreadsheet or notepad, or a more complex system, but either way you must ensure that no client falls through the cracks of communication.

We recommend you have a system in place either for your own benefit or for the benefit of the employee(s) who will be dealing with your customer communication.

1. Email received

2. Send response as quickly as possible (or an automated response) acknowledging you've received the email. If it's within your power to answer immediately, do so.

3. If you need to complete research for the answer or if an employee needs to ask you, have them mark down on your business calendar (or other means of organization) the necessary reply date.

4. Reply to email or communication with answer and provide a phone contact number in case of additional questions. Go above and beyond in this step.

5. If appropriate, send a follow up email that request feedback on your assistance.

For some small businesses, these steps may seem unnecessary (and in some cases they will be) but it's better to go above and beyond in your customer service by being organized and quick to respond. Don't forget clients or lose business due to lack of organization in this area.

Marketing and Promotion

Timing is everything. There have been various studies done regarding social media and the best times to post during the day as well as weekly. It's important that you pay close attention to these things and organize you posts to maximize your impact.

1. Establish *what* you will post.
    Decide the content and images that are important to share with your online community and choose what you will post of them (keeping an eye toward the tone of voice you use).
2. Figure out *when* you should post.
    This will require some research into the

studies we have mentioned but an easy Google search should provide you with a few info graphics that are easy to understand. Use these to figure out how many posts to schedule, when to schedule them, and where.

3. Schedule your posts.
   This last part is what will take the longest time. Using helpful sites like HootSuite or TweetDeck allows you to schedule out posts in advance, but we recommend making these posts as unique as possible. This does take more time, but the response will be noticeable.

Staying on top of your social media posting is crucial to your small business, especially if you are not in a position to spend a lot on marketing or promotion. Use good quality images, intriguing text, and short links to draw your viewers in.

On-site

This is likely the most obvious use of organization. It can often take additional work on the front end to create spaces that are conducive to your work style, but it is an integral part of organizing your business. A well-ordered work space not only helps you to stay on task and find things quickly, but it can also be conducive to the creative process.

Start by asking these questions and considering their applications:

What do I need organized?

There are all different types of things that need to be organized like papers, supplies, and products. When you stand in the space that needs to be organized you may want to take one of two approaches:

1. Visualize new ways to organize the space

2. Clear everything away and reorder it as you clean

Some people have the ability to see a space for its potential; others need to see a clean slate. Whatever your preference, make sure you carve out enough time in order to begin and end the process of cleaning and reorganizing. While reorganizing, take into account the items you need ready access to. These things should be easy to reach, close to your desk, and logically organized for easy reference. If you require access to files, make sure you decide on how you will alphabetize and stick to that decision.

How do I want to organize it?

As you are looking at your space, you must also decide on how you want to organize. In some cases you won't have many options due to space or the type of items being organized. Other times, you may be able to make choices based on color code, alphabetical, or size. Choose the system that works best for you and then stick with it.

Smart Idea: If you make a unilateral decision to change the way you organize, notify anyone involved with keeping that space organized. Do a quick introduction or training if time allows so that everyone is informed.

Financial

This is a specific type of organization that takes tools and systems to be in place in order to make that organization effective. No matter the size of your business, you will need to have a place to file receipts, tax info, and other important financial papers. If your business is rapidly growing, you may want to invest in a bookkeeping program or hire a part time bookkeeper. That is a type of organizational delegation that will prove to be beneficial for your time and when it comes to taxes.

Technological

The last area to think through in regards to organization for your small business is technology. It is sometimes easier to keep a space organized than it is digital files. You can physically see when something is out of place in your office, but you can't always see when your files are mixed up on your hard drive.

It's worth it to create a filing system that works well for you. If you're using folders on your hard drive, make sure that they are accurately labeled. It is also a good idea, especially considering taxes, to keep finical and tax records in dated folders labeled per year.

Whatever system you choose, make sure it is easily understandable, that you can find everything you need quickly, and that you keep up on your digital records as you would physical ones. They may not take up space like tangible files do, but they can clutter your desk top or sit in an uncategorized file which then is a hassle when you need to find a particular file.

All of these tips and tricks are aimed at creating an organized space (physical and digital) that frees you up to run your business in the most efficient manner possible. Putting these things into place early on will save you time and energy later, when you will need it the most.

Chapter 4. The Why: Why Time Management Is Important For Small Business Owners

We've looked at why organization is important to small businesses, but we'd like to point out the fact that organization only goes so far if you don't have other time management steps in place. You can be organized in every way but still find yourself stressed, overworked, and behind. None of this creates a healthy and pleasing atmosphere for work or for potential customers and clients.

Taking the Time for Time Management

When asked about how your business is going, your first response shouldn't be "I don't have time for myself." This may be true in the early, start up stages, but the longer you are in business the better your time should be managed an allocated appropriately.

Sometimes the difficulty of time management is the fact that it takes *time* to evaluate where and how you spend your time. Below, we'll take a look at four areas of importance when it comes to time management within your small business. These are the "whys" when considering time management.

You Only Have One Life

Take a moment to stop and evaluate yourself, your business, and your time. Remember the question we asked before? "Is it possible to live a fulfilling life as a small business owner?" Here is where your answer to that question comes into play. Since we all only have one life to live, we need to make sure every moment counts.

Smart Idea Exercise:

Take a moment to draw a pie chart. Start by dividing up your time into percentages (out of 100%) according to these areas:

- Work (your small business)
- Rest (sleep)
- Family
- Learning
- Fun and relaxation

Be honest with your evaluation. Then draw an open circle and put a point in the middle. From there, draw a line to the outer line. Now, as accurately as possible, divide up your chart according to your percentages listed above.

What does your chart look like? What slice of your pie is the largest? The answer to this question tells you how you have oriented your priorities.

Now, try this again with the categories from above. Write out what you would *like* your pie to look like (an "ideal" situation). This "ideal pie" is now your goal. You should, of course, determine if the allocations are realistic, but if they are, then consider what changes you need to make in order to move your "current pie" toward your "ideal" one. This could take years to achieve, but you now have a goal to aim for.

You Should Be Multiplying Your Time

Everyone loves a system that, once you get it to work, it does so seamlessly and without additional effort. Unfortunately, those types of systems don't tend to come about organically and generally take a lot of work to set up.

When you spend time focusing on implementing good time management skills, you can do so with an eye toward multiplying your time. A great example of this type of multiplication is scheduling out social media posts in advance. They are technically "working" for you throughout the week without you having to spend the time every day. Now, this does take an investment of time on the outset, but it reaps benefits long into the week (or month, depending on how far you schedule ahead).

You should always be looking for ways to multiply your time for the least amount of effort possible. It's not about being lazy but working smart.

Eliminate Stress

Managing your time well means eliminating stress, or at least greatly reducing it. You will create a better quality of work, have more energy for what matters, and an all-around healthier outlook when you aren't working under stress. This, in and of itself, will create a better work environment, but it will also create a more productive environment. Working with little to no stress means you are able to enjoy your work. This can lead to greater innovation as well as a brighter outlook on your business.

Be More Efficient

Everyone is given the same twenty-four hours in day. It's what we do with those hours that count. Efficiency is an important aspect of time management for your small business.

To help get an accurate picture of your time, list out these things:

- **What tasks do I need to complete?**
  Think: daily, weekly, monthly, quarterly, yearly, bi-yearly

- **How long should these tasks take?**
  Give an estimation on how long these takes *should* take (not how long they actually do)

- **What would I like to add on to this routine?**
  Think: goals, dreams, new products/services

Now, looking at this list, write in how long these tasks *actually* take. You may need to do this over the course of a week while you evaluate your time spent. What you will notice as you map out your actual time versus your preconceived time, is that there are a lot more interruptions on your time than you actually plan for. This is natural, but also probably throws off your time estimations.

The goal here is to gain an appropriate picture of what your time really looks like, not how you view your time looking on a "perfect" day. This helps with efficiency because, if you can see how your time is actually spent, you can schedule more accurately and plan in time for interruptions. You can also avoid feeling less productive by making your to-do list appropriate for your allotted time.

This type of efficiency helps you to look at what *is* instead of what *could* be. Being realistic about your time is the first step toward time management.

Time management is crucial to your business, no matter if you are the sole worker or the boss of several. You must be able to manage you own time well in accordance with others time, whether that's your employees or your customers. Take a look at the next chapter for tips and tricks of practical applications to hone your time management skills.

Chapter 5. Small Business Time Management Tips and Tricks

After seeing the importance of managing you time well, we'll now take a look at some easily implemented tips and tricks to make the most of your time. These things, as with organizational ideas, aren't a cure-all. You still need to put in the hard work of evaluating what does and doesn't work as well as making appropriate adjustments to adapt these tips to your personal situation.

It's About You

The benefit of being a small business owner is that your business reflects you. That means your organization and time management needs to do the same. We understand that not every small business owner has the ability to craft their time in the way they would ultimately like. However, to the extent that you can, it is important that you manage your time to what suits you and your customer's best. It may seem selfish, but consider the fact that what makes your business successful is ultimately you. This revolves around the customer, but the idea (the "heart") comes from you. Take that into consideration.

Find Your Prime Time

As we've said, your small business is, in essence, about you. You may not have the ability to move your working hours around, depending on your business, but you do have the luxury to work your free time around what best fits with your internal schedule. Some people work well in the morning, others late at night, but no matter when your *prime time* is, you need to be working during that time!

Depending on your business hours, plan your schedule according to that and your prime time. Use that prime time to brainstorm business ideas, get creative about problem solving, or work on organization. Whatever the most pressing need for your business is, use your prime time toward that effort. In conjunction with the rest of these tips and tricks, you will have more energy and a better focus during that time.

Also consider the best use of your prime time. If you have a morning commute, find a way to make that commute useful. You could be brainstorming ideas to a voice recorder, listening to an audio book for small business, or completing phone calls through Bluetooth during this time. Don't let parts of your workday slip by unused. It's important to use work time well, so that when you have free time you don't feel the need to still be working.

Smart Idea: Weather it's at six a.m. or eleven p.m., use your prime time to work on the innovative portions of your business. When you're at your best, you're inclined to be more creative and to produce your best work.

Before You Start

The most important time for you as a small business owner is the start of your day (whenever this may be). Use this time to sit down and plot out your to-do list. Remember our previous point about efficiency and be realistic with your time, but write it all out. It may be useful to have a white board above your desk or some other type of visual aid just so you know what you're doing and when.

At this point, depending on how your day typically pans out, it may be helpful to write in action items by time block. If your job is more fluid, then just write out tasks, but we would encourage you to be intentional with prioritizing the items. Some things should be non-negotiable that need to be accomplished that day; others can be bumped to the next day, but don't make this a habit.

Smart Idea: If you are constantly moving action items to the next day, you are overestimating your time in the day. Scale back what you need to accomplish. This is important because, at the end of the day, you don't want to feel as if you haven't accomplished things. This can lead to a type of depression and isn't actually an accurate picture of what you are accomplishing on a daily basis.

Use a Timer

There are times to ignore the clock and there are times to put it to good use. Make sure you know the difference!

After you've taken time to plan out your day and prioritize, use a time to spur your creativity. Multi-tasking is great, but studies show that you don't accomplish as much when your focus is divided. Plan out your tasks for the day and set aside chunks of time toward each large task.

Once you've chosen a task, use a timer to allot time to that task, and *focus*. When the timer goes off, evaluate your progress. If you finish, great! If not, estimate how much more time you'll need and weight you options. If you can reallocate time from another project, do so. If not, either leave that project to the end of your work day or move it to the top of your to-do list for the next day. This helps you learn and practice discipline with your tasks.

Smart Idea: Start implementing the use of a timer with the strict idea that, whatever you don't fit into your allotted time frames must be moved to the next day. This helps to shape your boundary lines for your business. You'll start to find that a) you plan your time better and b) the world won't end if you don't get to that last project (usually).

Take Away Distractions

In today's world this idea is extremely difficult. There is always another email to be answers, call to take, texts to reply to, or Facebook messages coming in. It is easy to get distracted by the little things and realize they take up most of your time. Establish a precedent now with regards to guarding your dedicated work time. Turn your phone to "do not disturb" (so your timer will still work but you won't be distracted), close out of your email, and don't open Facebook except for your scheduled times.

Working a solid hour without distraction will improve the quality of your work as well as the pace at which you can finish your work. Overall, you will feel more accomplished after this. Though emails are important (especially with regards to customer service) you will find that they take up a lot of time. Be smart about scheduling in time to answer emails, return calls and texts, and to check your social media.

Plan to Be Social

It may seem ridiculous to plan time to be on social media, but if it's not planned, then that's time taken away from another area of your priorities list. When you plan in your time on Facebook, Twitter, Instagram, and Pinterest, you automatically go in with the idea that this is in association with work, not pleasure.

This is important for things like social media because they can become large time wasters. You will find yourself scrolling through endless feeds on Facebook, completely forgetting why you were on there in the first place.The same can be said for blog reading for research. This is a good action and you can gain knowledge from it, but you must be cautious of how easy it is to waste time doing what appears to be helpful but is in fact a distraction. Use a timer while on social media and make sure it is part of your scheduled day.

Smart Idea: Consider breaking up these media times into ten or fifteen minute increments throughout the day. This will keep you "current" without overtaking your day.

Rest Up

There needs to be a large emphasis on rest when considering your time management. This is important because no one is a machine. Being human means there is a deep-seated need for rest and taking breaks. This is becoming increasingly more important as research shows that standing for portions of the day (if you work at a desk) can help improve your health as well as your productivity.

While planning out your day, include times for adequate breaks. This includes ten to fifteen minute breaks as well as a lunch break. During these breaks make sure you stand up, stretch, and actually rest. Stepping away from a project can help improve your perspective and stamina when you come back to it. Just make sure you leave any project or work with clearly defined notes as to where you're heading next. There's nothing worse than walking away and not remembering your direction after the break.

Smart Idea: Combine a few of these tips! Take your social media and rest breaks while standing near or at your desk. Don't do this for every break, but occasionally.

Own Up to It

The last thing to consider when focusing on time management is to understand the reality that sometimes you cannot accomplish everything you want to. You may have had the best of intentions when setting out to create you priority list for the day or week, but planning for the unplanned is hard enough without being able to keep up with your normal day-to-day business requirements.

Allow yourself a bit of slack when it comes to accomplishing your goals. As we've already stated, if you find you are constantly overestimating the amount of work you will finish or underestimating the amount of time it will take to complete a task, reevaluate. This is not admitting defeat; it's a smart business move.

This may also mean adjusting your overall goals. If you've set certain goals for the next six months but are realizing they may not be possible, adjust for that. What is most important is that you do the best you can with the things you already have in place before adding anything to your schedule or your business.

Time management takes time to plan out, but in the end you will reap the benefits for having set aside that time. Be through and use helpful tools like timers, spreadsheets, and online time-trackers to ensure you are making the best use of your time. At the end of the day, don't mourn the incomplete tasks, but give yourself credit for what you *did* accomplish. Use those unfinished tasks to fuel your next day's to-do list.

Lastly, you will likely find that, when you track your time, your unproductive hours are spent on things that don't add to your relaxation or overall well-being. Use your free time to spend with your family and friends, working out and eating healthy, and spending time actually resting. You will feel more rejuvenated for having spent an actual day of than spending half an hour here and there taking a break.

Chapter 6. Goal Planning and Future Organization for Small Businesses

We've looked at the importance of organization and time management for small business, but within these two areas we touched a little on establishing goals and thinking through the extent of your organization. We'll spend just a little additional time here on these two things as they relate to organization and optimizing your time management.

Goals Worth Achieving

After a business plan has been created, business goals are next in line of importance to the forward motion of your business. Without clearly defined goals coming out of identified strengths and weaknesses of your business as it is now, you won't be moving forward. This can be intimidating, establishing the future of your business, but it is crucial for forward movement. Don't worry though; long-term goals, though firm, don't have to be a completely set in stone idea. They can, however, create a healthy motion for your business.

We recommend you set aside at least half a day if not longer to goal-plan for your future. This should come after you've established your business plan. You'll want to have paper or a white board handy to map out the trajectory of your business.

Walk through these steps:

1. **Start with your business plan and tagline.**

   Take a few minutes to remind yourself of why you started your business in the first place, the "heart". This is the essence of you business and should fuel everything you do. If it isn't true to where your business is today, adjust it to fit the new perspective. It is important to keep this up-to-date.

   In some cases this could mean rebranding. In others, just a re-focusing of priorities.

2. **Brainstorm/Think ahead.**

   It's time to do a little dreaming. This is a great opportunity to let your imagination run wild. Don't restrict yourself to what you *think* is possible but what you would like to be possible. This is a crucial step because it takes away the societal and realized boundaries and instead lets you see what you actually hope for.

3. **Narrow your focus.**

   Take the things you brainstormed, organize them, and start to weed out things that either aren't likely to happen or are not possible within the next five years. These aren't completely taken out of the realm of possibility, but they aren't factors at this point either (possibly due to money, time, or other constraints).

4. **Map it out.**

   Now, take the things from your narrowed focus and begin to organize them into realistic categories depending on how far out you think they will need to be planned. If you currently run a small store and wish to have a chain of five up and running in the future, you wouldn't put that goal a year away. That's upwards of a five to ten year goal. Just make sure you are realistic about these plans.

5. **Get specific.**

This is very important when it comes to goal creation. If you aren't specific to the goal, its needs in order to be reached, and a plan as to how you will get there, you aren't likely to reach that goal. Work from the outward in (years wise) and become more and more detailed the closer you get to where you are at right now. The closer out each goal is, the more steps you should create. Don't make these steps so impossible that you are never achieving them. Some will naturally be harder, but be sure to be realistic to.

6. **Work your goals.**

    This is the part where you get to implement your goals and the steps to achieving them. This may require a directional change of your business, daily routine changes, or even reallocation of time and/or money to achieve these goals. Do these things with your goals clearly in mind.

Make sure to schedule regular check-ups to see how you are doing with relation to your goals. Are your timelines realistic? Are you feeling overwhelmed by what you have chosen to accomplish? Are your goals too easy? Make the time to reevaluate and adjust as necessary.

Smart Planning

We can talk a lot about planning, but if it's not smart planning, it will only be a waste of time.

What we mean by smart planning is that it is concise, cost effective, takes into account your tagline or business focus, and doesn't take over your time. When you goal plan, you can get wrapped up in the future of you business and forsake the current state of it. That will only bring trouble in the present and the future.

When you plan ahead for your business, make sure your plans are leading you toward a goal and aren't so difficult to implement that you or your customers become frustrated. The difficulty in planning and organizing is that it will affect your customers during the adjustment time to a new system. If changes are made that affect your customers, be sure to inform them along the way of new policies, procedures, prices, and practices. Be careful to care for them during this time so that they aren't feeling left behind with regards to any new direction or idea.

It's important to note here that any changes put into place should consider your customer. The marketing aspect of your business should afford you a good look into what your clientele likes and wants. Any change you make should be in line with that.

Better Organization

For every organizational procedure put in place, there are positives and negatives. The discussion of the best future organization centers on the fact that you won't know if your organizational systems are working until you put them in place and allow them to do just that, work. We've talked a lot about reevaluating, but that's not just a buzzword. You have to allow time for a system to fall into working order before seeing its results.

Now, obviously you won't want to let a failed system go on failing just to meet a stated time-goal, but you should make sure to give adequate time to see the ups and downs. There will likely need to be small adjustments made, but let your system fall into place before deciding if it works or not.

Once you've given it adequate time (anywhere from three to six months) reevaluate. Are the systems you put in place working? What's meeting your needs? What isn't? What's wrong? What's working well?

Ask these questions then consider future systems you may want to put into place. Maybe that's additional shelving, relabeling everything, or a total remodel of your space. These things may not be crucial, but they are good to consider in addition to new ways to keep your spaces organized. Leave room for growth while still making sure that what you have in place is doing a good job.

Being a small business owner, you are constantly faced with the reality of the here and now. There are challenges you must over come without having to consider your organizational skills or time management, but neglecting their importance is a big mistake. Just a little time spent organizing your space and time will greatly increase your productivity while decreasing your stress. This will not only affect you and your personal stress level, but also the relationships you will have with your clients.

Realize that you absolutely *can* live a fulfilling and relaxed life as a small business owner by taking the proper precautions on your time. Step into better organization and time management today, and realize a brighter future for your business tomorrow.